HEROES OF AMERICAN HISTORY

Laura Bush
First Lady

Carmen Bredeson

Enslow Publishers, Inc.

40 Industrial Road   PO Box 38
Box 398   Aldershot
Berkeley Heights, NJ 07922   Hants GU12 6BP
USA   UK

http://www.enslow.com

Library of Congress Cataloging-in-Publication Data

Bredeson, Carmen.
    Laura Bush : first lady / Carmen Bredeson.
        v. cm. — (Heroes of American history)
    Contents: Books and teaching—Marriage and family—First Lady of Texas—First Lady of the United States—Disaster strikes America.
    Includes Index.
    ISBN 0-7660-2101-7 (hardcover)
    1. Bush, Laura Welch, 1946–   .—Juvenile literature. 2. Presidents' spouses—United States—Biography—Juvenile literature. [1. Bush, Laura Welch, 1946–   . 2. First Ladies.] I. Title. II. Series.
    E904.B87 B74   2002
    973.931'092—dc21

                                                    2002000490

J
92
Bush

Printed in the United States of America

10 9 8 7 6 5 4 3 2 1

To Our Readers: We have done our best to make sure all Internet Addresses in this book were active and appropriate when we went to press. However, the author and the publisher have no control over and assume no liability for the material available on those Internet sites or on other Web sites they may link to. Any comments or suggestions can be sent by e-mail to comments@enslow.com or to the address on the back cover.

Every effort has been made to locate all copyright holders of material used in this book. If any errors or omissions have occurred, corrections will be made in future editions of this book.

Illustration Credits: AP/Wide World Photos, pp. 3, 4, 8, 16, 18, 19, 21, 22, 24, 25, 26–27, 28; Classmates.com, p. 7; © Corel Corporation, pp. 1, 2, 17; Department of Defense, www.defenselink.mil, p. 4; George Bush Presidential Library, pp. 10, 11, 12, 13, 15; Simon Rosenstein, p. 6.

Cover Credits: AP/Wide World Photos

Table of Contents

Laura Welch Bush

Chapter 1

Books and Teaching

Laura Welch decided to become a teacher when she was in the second grade. She liked to line up her dolls and play school. Her students were very quiet as Laura read some of her favorite books aloud.

As a girl, Laura never dreamed that she would grow up to be the first lady of the United States.

Laura was born on November 4, 1946, in the small, friendly town of Midland, Texas. She was the only child of Harold B. Welch, a home builder, and Jenna Welch. When she was still a tiny baby, her mother started reading to her. As Laura grew, she and her mother took many trips to the library. Laura loved the *Little House on the Prairie* books, by Laura Ingalls Wilder.

Laura was always reading.

At James Bowie Elementary School in Midland, Laura was quiet, but she had many friends. Laura sang in the choir, played the piano, and belonged to the Brownie Scouts.

In junior high and high school, Laura earned good grades. On weekends, she and her friends enjoyed listening to records, driving around town, and going to football games. Laura graduated from high school in 1964.

At Southern Methodist University in Dallas, Texas, Laura studied to become a teacher. When she graduated in 1968, she took a job teaching second grade in Austin, Texas. Laura often went outside at recess and played with her students. They liked that. Her students also liked the extra help she gave them with their schoolwork.

Laura taught elementary school for several years. Then she decided to become a librarian. Laura loved books and reading. She wanted to help young people learn to love reading, too. In 1973, when she was in her mid-twenties, Laura earned a master's degree in library science from the University of Texas at Austin.

Laura worked in a public

Laura's high school yearbook picture.

As a little girl, Laura often read stories to her dolls.
As a grown-up, she loves reading to children.

library for one year, but she missed being with young children. So she became a school librarian.

When students came into the library looking for a special book, Miss Welch was happy to help them. She liked reading books to classes of students and teaching them how to do research to find facts.

Chapter 2

Marriage and Family

During her summer vacation in 1977, Laura went home to Midland for a visit. There, she was invited to a backyard barbecue. Her friends wanted her to meet someone. It was George W. Bush.

George and Laura liked each other right away. Laura liked George's sense of humor. He made her laugh. George told his friends that Laura was smart and pretty. He was drawn to her steady, calm

Laura and George, on their wedding day

personality. On November 5, 1977, just three months after they met, George W. Bush and Laura Welch were married. They were both thirty-one years old.

The couple lived in Midland, Texas, where George worked for an oil company. But he had bigger plans for his life. George was interested in government. He hoped to be elected to the United States Congress. In the months before the election, George and Laura talked to many voters. They told the people of Midland that he would be a good congressman.

In spite of their hard work, George Bush did not win the election. So he stayed in the oil business.

George's father, George Herbert Walker (H.W.)

Bush, also wanted to help run the government of the United States. In 1980, he was elected vice president of the country, serving under President Ronald Reagan. Vice President and Mrs. Bush now lived in Washington, D.C.

Back in Texas, Laura and George W. Bush were eager to have a family. On November 25, 1981, their dream came true. Twin daughters, Jenna and Barbara, were born. Laura left her school library job to

The couple drove around Texas, asking people to vote for George.

Laura, the twins, and George W. with
his mother, Barbara Bush.

take care of the babies. She loved cuddling her little
girls and reading books to them.

After being vice president for eight years, George's
dad hoped to become president. George, Laura, and
the twins moved to Washington, D.C., to help him
win votes. In 1988, when the twins were almost seven
years old, their grandfather was elected president of
the United States. Their grandmother was now the

first lady. George H. W. Bush and his wife, Barbara, moved into the White House. Laura, George W., and their children returned to Texas.

With the oil business slowing down, George W. decided to sell his oil company. He had always loved baseball. Now he became part owner of the Texas Rangers, a major-league baseball team. George, Laura, and the twins moved to Dallas, Texas. It was fun going to baseball games and talking to the players. The Bushes liked watching the games from the dugout.

The whole Bush family enjoys getting together in Maine.

Chapter 3

First Lady of Texas

George W. Bush did not forget his interest in government. In 1993, when he was forty-seven years old, he ran for governor of Texas. On Election Day, the people of Texas voted him into office.

Laura Bush was now the first lady of Texas, an important person in the state. She and her family moved into the governor's mansion in Austin.

People wanted to know Laura's opinions about

everything. At first Laura was shy about giving speeches. She was not used to talking to big crowds. But soon she grew more comfortable. People listened closely when she spoke.

Laura saw a way to use her love of books to help others. There are many adults and children in America who cannot read. Laura helped raise money for programs that teach people to read. These are called literacy programs. A person who is literate is one who can read.

Vacations are fun for a busy family like the Bushes.

15

Creating the Texas Book Festival was one of Laura Bush's special projects. It is now held each year at the Texas State Capitol in Austin. Authors read from their books in different rooms of the building. Colorful tents are set up outside. Some are for booksellers. In other tents, musical groups, clowns, and storytellers perform. The money raised by the festival is given to Texas libraries.

As first lady of Texas, Laura Bush was busy in her office every day. She answered mail and worked on projects to support literacy and breast cancer research. She was also proud to show off the work of

Victory! George W. won the race for governor of Texas.

Texas artists. She displayed their paintings on the walls of her office.

With her work and her family, Laura Bush did not have very much free time. To relax, she liked to work in her garden. Laura belonged to a garden club in Austin. She enjoyed sharing ideas with other people who loved plants and flowers.

Laura Bush spent six years as the first lady of Texas. During that time, Jenna and Barbara grew into young ladies. They finished high school in Austin, and then it was time for college. Jenna decided to attend the University of Texas, and Barbara picked Yale University.

Their dad was also making a big decision. Another presidential election was coming up in the year 2000. Should George W. Bush follow in his father's footsteps and try to be president of the United States?

In 1999, Laura and George rode in a parade to celebrate his reelection as governor of Texas.

The family spent a lot of time talking about this. Being president is a very hard job. Laura and the twins also worried that they would lose their privacy. Reporters and cameras would always be around.

After talking about it for a long time, the whole family agreed that George W. Bush should enter the race. This meant months on the road for George and Laura. They traveled all across America to talk to people. They wanted voters to meet George W. and hear his plans for America. Laura was at his side, shaking hands and giving speeches.

Laura helped her husband win votes.

George W. Bush was running against Vice President Al Gore. Each man wanted to be the president, but only one of them could win.

Chapter 4

First Lady of the United States

Americans went to the polls on Election Day, November 7, 2000, to cast their votes. The election was very close, and it was not clear who won. There were questions about the votes in Florida. Several weeks passed while the votes were counted and recounted.

At last, George Walker Bush was declared the winner of the election. On January 20, 2001, he became president of the United States. Laura Welch Bush became the first lady.

Laura's first job was to help her family settle into the White House. Barbara and Jenna were away at college, but the Bushes had their pets to keep them company. Their two dogs, Spot and Barney, and India the cat were a little nervous. They ran around sniffing and exploring their new house.

Barbara, left, and Jenna are proud of their famous parents.

The White House is not an ordinary home. It has 132 rooms! On the ground floor are the kitchen, laundry, and offices. There are also five rooms that are open to the public, such as the State Dining Room and Blue Room. The first family lives on the second floor. The third floor has rooms for guests and some staff members. In the basement are a bowling alley and a movie theater.

First Lady Laura Bush is very busy in her office in the White House. As first lady, she brings national attention to issues that are important to her.

The new first lady wants all Americans to know how to read.

On September 8, 2001, Mrs. Bush held the first National Book Festival. She invited authors and storytellers to the nation's capital. Children lined up to have their pictures taken with Clifford the Big Red Dog and other book characters.

In her job as first lady, Laura Bush promised to work hard for literacy, education, and medical research, just as she did in Texas.

Chapter 5

Disaster Strikes America

On September 11, 2001, Laura Bush was on her way to a meeting. She was planning to give a speech at the United States Senate. She would talk to the senators about children and reading.

Then she heard some terrible news. Two planes had crashed into the World Trade Center towers in New York City. A third plane slammed into the Pentagon in Washington, D.C., and a fourth plane

Laura Bush talked to schoolchildren about hatred and misunderstanding among people.

crashed in Pennsylvania. Terrorists were attacking America.

Secret Service agents rushed Mrs. Bush to a safe location. Their job is to protect the president and his family. President Bush, who was in Florida at the time of the attacks, hurried back to the government.

Americans were very upset after September 11. Laura Bush visited schools to talk to children about what had happened. She listened to their fears and tried to help them feel safe. The first lady also visited with families who had lost loved ones. She was very sad that more than 3,000 Americans had died in the attacks.

In November, Laura Bush gave a speech on the radio. The president usually talked to the nation on Saturdays, but he gave the radio time to his wife instead. The first lady talked about the terrible ways that women are treated in some countries around the world.

There are places where women and girls have no rights. They are not allowed to go to school or to vote.

Mrs. Bush is the only first lady in history to give the president's weekly radio speech.

They cannot hold important jobs in the government. Laura Bush called upon world leaders to help these women.

The U.S. government worried that more terrorists might try to attack America. Because of that, security was increased around the nation. The White House canceled all tours during the Christmas holidays in 2001. The public would not be allowed to enter the White House.

Instead, the first lady took Americans on a television tour of the house. Forty-nine fir trees were beautifully decorated in white. In the State

Dining Room was a gingerbread house that weighed 130 pounds. It was a copy of the White House as it looked in 1800, the year it was built.

On January 24, 2002, the first lady gave a speech in the Senate. This was the one that she had planned to give on September 11. Mrs. Bush talked to the senators about the importance of reading. Students with poor reading skills have a hard time in school. Some even decide to quit. Without a high school education, they have trouble getting good jobs. Mrs. Bush asked the senators to support better programs for schools.

Being first lady of the United States keeps Laura

This is one of the White House Christmas trees in 2001.

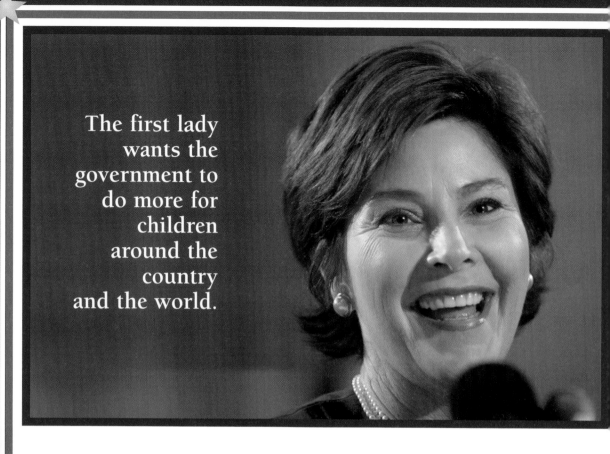

The first lady wants the government to do more for children around the country and the world.

Bush very busy. She visits schools, gives speeches, and raises money for important causes.

Since moving into the White House, Mrs. Bush has worked hard for children, for education, and for women's health. The United States is facing new and difficult challenges. First Lady Laura Bush will do all she can to help the American people.

Timeline

1946~Laura Lane Welch is born in Midland, Texas, on November 4.

1964~Graduates from Lee High School in Midland.

1968~Graduates from Southern Methodist University. Begins teaching second grade.

1973~Earns a master's degree in library science from the University of Texas.

1977~Marries George W. Bush.

1981~Twins Jenna and Barbara are born on November 25.

1994~Becomes first lady of Texas after George W. is elected governor.

1996~Starts the Texas Book Festival.

2001~Becomes first lady of the United States.

Words to Know

disaster—Something that causes great harm.

first lady—Title given to the wife of a governor or president.

hijack—To take control of a vehicle by force.

literacy—Being able to read and write.

master's degree—An advanced course of study for people who have finished college.

security—Protection from harm.

terrorist—Someone who causes great fear, usually through violence.

U.S. Congress—The lawmaking arm of the government. It has two parts, the Senate and the House of Representatives.

U.S. congressman—A lawmaker in the House of Representatives.

U.S. senator—A lawmaker in the Senate.

Learn More

Books

Sanders, Mark. *The White House*. Austin, Tex.: Steadwell Books, 2000.

Stone, Tanya Lee. *Laura Welch Bush: First Lady*. Brookfield, Conn.: Millbrook Press, 2001.

Wade, Mary Dodson. *George W. Bush*. Austin, Tex.: W. S. Benson and Co., 2002.

Internet Addresses

The White House for Kids
<http://www.whitehouse.gov/kids/firstlady>

Laura Bush at the White House
<http://www.whitehouse.gov/firstlady>

Index